The Naked Prince

The Naked Prince

NEW & SELECTED POEMS

Ben Greer

Press 53

Winston-Salem

Press 53, LLC
PO Box 30314
Winston-Salem, NC 27130

First Edition

Cover art, "Linear Abstract Faces," Copyright © 2019
by Komarova Anastasiia
Licensed through iStock

Cover design by Christopher Forrest

Library of Congress Control Number
2020946566

Printed on acid-free paper
ISBN 978-1-950413-27-0

For H.A.Maxson:
we made our lives among these fickle lines—
I hold only to you.

Acknowledgments

Thank you to the editors of the publications where many of these poems first appeared, including *Delaware Poetry Review, Georgetown Review, James Dickey Newsletter, Main Channel Voices, Prairie Schooner, Runes: A Review of Poetry, The Sewanee Review, The South Carolina Review, Southern Poetry Anthology, The Southern Review, The Texas Review, University of Virginia Press,* and *Winning Writers Review.*

Additional thanks to those who helped along the way, especially Shaye Areheart, Fred Chappell, Billy Collins, Kwame Dawes, James Dickey, Annie Dillard, Richard Dillard, George and Susan Garrett, X.J. Kennedy, William Jay Smith, Henry Taylor, and Richard Wilbur.

Special thanks to Christopher Forrest and Kevin Morgan Watson of Press 53 for their belief in me and my work.

Contents

The Naked Prince

The Naked Prince

No child had a grander view:
New York City sixty floors up
in Douglas Edwards' apartment.
Dad was interviewing
with Mister Paley for a job.

I was five, I think. Mother
stood me on the anchor's
couch, naked with a golden
crown of paper on my head
and said: Here it is.

This is what you must take.
Take it or come back home and learn
the secrets of stick shifts or toilets
or lawnmowers.
Be a king or nothing.

Quilt

A quarrel. Loud and bungling.
We are standing before the new window
Susan built in the den. Outside lies
the winter hedge trimmed hard.

I don't remember the subject,
something about my demeanor.
Afterwards, hushed bruising until you say,
"Let's go see the quilt show."

We jump into the yellow
Jeep convertible hunting for
St. John the demure hidden

among firs and pines near cold
sea inlets above which ravel
blue tatters of fog.

Following signs nailed to birches
and birches alone, we find a driveway,
turn, and give the car gas until it lurches

over the hill. Below, a hundred
or more white and yellow gravestones
stand like a damp, toddling army

protecting the little church we enter.
Hundreds of quilts glimmer in the vestibule,
their colors nacreous as the wings of

jungle birds. You lead me through the maple
pews and stop before an altar
over which hangs one quilt

different from the rest: thin,
ragged, a drained complexion,
peeling with tears and patches.

You look at me:
"There," you say. "That's the way
it must be."

A First Memory

Ripe with sleep
only a car can make,
I hear my father's voice
like a cat's breath,
feel his arms
scoop me from
a vinyl seat
in the old Chevy.
I relax
in his embrace
and the doting night.

Feeling, even then, feeling
this is love: carried
towards the windows of home
by the first man to know
me, loose and languid
beneath
the humpty dumpty moon.

Mentor

I would rather have life this way:
        an endless wood for boys.
Not the gaudy woods summer brings,
        with cockades and festoons of leaves.
Rather let the trees be stripped and clear
        so boys can see the best one.
Single this tree out and rush it hard
        halfway up with a kick.
Then find themselves in stillness plotting
        their way across the limbs.
Crawling around a ball of green
        mistletoe, or stopping
to search some abandoned nest littered
        with blue and speckled shells.
Out of breath and biceps aching,
        they spot the summit limb,
but dare themselves even more,
        reaching for the invisible,
lusting beyond their grip:
        some dream   some prize
        some stinging triumph.

A Boy in Guatemala

Dulier, I didn't tell you I was coming. I wanted it to be my secret. I found you on a dusty street in Tecpan. There was a festival. Baskets of corn and beans and tomatoes red as my heart for you piled the square. You were playing near your home where I send things. In your bright black shoes and new trousers.

Tolstoy said the only real joy in life is loving others. I stuck a bouquet of daisies in your soccer shoes and snuck away to the airport.

Digital Joy

He woke dreaming of scissors.
After he cut the hair
from his fingers, he found
it wasn't enough.
And so took the razor
to them. Suddenly there
they were—the fingers of youth:
scars, pepper birdshot, marble knuckles,
a ruddiness he had not seen
since he was twenty.

Bloom

A long time ago I saw angels coming
bright with keys. I was not shaving then.
My cheeks, camellias, white in the bloom.
Time came begging. I never thought it could be so
hungry, so ready to gorge itself with me.

I still believe the angels are coming
and they are bright, but not with keys.
They stand before
my locked door, holding
a starry axe.

The House

Out of that monstrous, galloping, gorgeous endless edifice a
dream swells I am with someone upstairs the tall windows
are open but my bedroom is black I don't remember the
other kid only he is a friend we are listening to something
outside near the stairs we're afraid looking at the gnarled
door to see if it's locked the key is like a thin blue bone we
hear clicking on the wooden floor in the grand hall the
fever heart of this house a sound claws make something
pacing, almost frantically pacing by the door waiting to
get inside waiting to get us something like an animal my
friend is terrified he asks: what is it? I answer in maniacal
giddiness, almost laughing oh don't worry I know I know
what it is he looks at me why do I make him wait? Benny,
what's out there, man?

Mama, I say it's just my Mama.

Practice at Fort Jackson

When air is heavy,
the big mortars boom and grunt
against the low clouds.

Children learn to kill
on soft, gray spring days among
the white pear blossoms.

The Professor in Fall

I met you fall semester,
all blond and brown and young.
The bracelet on your ankle
was water to my tongue.

Not yet an old man crumbling
but close enough to age
to buy the last delusion:
the years have left me sage.

How this peregrination
will turn out in the end
makes no lasting difference:
I'm young, still young again.

Nothing Left Behind

In the country when I see posts
in a straight line along the road,
I sometimes stop to study
the farmer's craft: putting up wire
to make his field separate from
others. Since I was a boy, I loved
this close inspection, to grab it,
the wood first and then the wire, shaking
both to see if there was any give.
Then propping a foot below and elbow
above, resting to look at the fence
running through the grass and the ditch,
climbing up the hill to disappear
among the dark trees and the light.
Such simple lines. Such good work.

Older now, I realize there's
nothing like that for me.
Oh, I tried to build some things,
struggled long to make them
real, but somehow they
never stood or ran in places
I would like to keep and come
back to see with a certain pride.
My work was always dream.

Mama's Wisdom

The best in man is beast
said my mother after
I found her in
the silver closet
sitting with hiked skirt
on the three-hundred-pound
naked plumber whose
greasy hands had
blackened her white
thighs.

For the World

for Kwame Dawes

I didn't hear them when they died
but I thought I felt something.
It was raining, a February
day as I sat in my office
watching the local news.
The announcer said they hit
the side wall of the building.
Calls were made to appropriate
experts. No one seemed to know
why. Immediately I thought
it has to be the black glass wall.
Somehow they could not see it.
But then there was the other thing
I knew and that I had known
since I was a boy. They were drunk
from the glistening red berries:
pyracantha grown winter fat.

I crossed the street where the dark
hospital stood. It looked as if
someone had thrown red roses
by the dozens against the glass—
a hundred cardinals lay shattered
in a blur. Some of them not dead,
feathers and wings trembling, broken
beaks agape in their freezing
bacchanal. Beneath umbrellas
a crowd stared at the agony.
I knew no one could do anything
to anesthetize this pain.

At home I found the secret box
where I kept them in a row.
I had many, each wrapped in
a silken sheath. Each as perfect
as any pure edge could be.

It was an old idea which
grew around the age of sex
that if I cut myself until
the blood ran down in warm ribbons
all other pain would lessen. All—
not just my own. The very
pain of the world would diminish
into balls of red cotton
which I hid beneath my bed.
Sleeping above the crimson host
I dreamed of healing
a million wounds.

Now I open the hidden silk
and slide the clear edge of the razor
against this belly for the world.

The Bright House

York Harbor, Maine, where the York River flows into the Atlantic Ocean

I have come back
to the white house
beside the York River.
October turns the leaves orange and black.
Rain
needles the reedy shallows.

You sit at a metal table
facing upriver, staring out
a window. I look the other way
toward the sea from my desk,
which you put here for me.
A fire hisses in the black stove.

I have my back to the coals,
but can feel the chill
from the ghosts who surround you. A cloud
of them so cold and wet
they threaten to extinguish
all the living here.

You are busy someplace
in Elizabethan England.
Occasionally I hear you
murmur a few words to Cecil.
Or is it Lord Grey, or perhaps even
Good Queen Bess, though you
rarely talk to her so I can hear.

The dead chorus of that age
mutters and peeps, and
you must fight to make sure
your words are not dictation. You dip
a black pen into an ink bottle,
quickly scratch words on a
yellow pad, for it is twilight

and you must get down as much as
possible before Susan calls us to cocktails
and a red roast with asparagus. I write
fast too because I think I should, though
I am posing. I am not driven, except
to get to bourbon and soda.

I hear you put down your pen and screw
the top onto the bottle. You wipe away
black bubbles from the nib and set it
down again. I follow all your actions:
you have made me an inker too. You stand,
open the door of the stove and blink
at the inferno, dreaming. I wait

in black sea air until you bounce down
the planks heading for the bright house
above. You have taught me the time
for musing.

Side by side, we step, listening
to close boats bumping
in the river.

Eulogy

1.

He was not technological—only a scruple away from
a quill. How incongruous that an email contained
the news of his death. Something else. When I read it,
my whole house bloomed.

The clogged faucets began to pour water abundant
and clear. The clacking air conditioner delivered
autumn in a hush. Blasted screen on the porch
repelled flies and mosquitoes. Shrieking hinges sighed.
Doors opened. Whatever in my domestic world was broken,
for his death mended.

My wife and I went to the store and bought two boxes of
wine. We needed to talk and weep into obliteration.
Before bed, I took as many pills as possible without
seeing him before I should, and wondered as I entered the world
which is not death, why something had not told me. Like a hackle
or a pain in a place it's never been; or a strange, beating note:
George Garrett is dead.
George is dead.
George.

Now all that I wanted to be I must become, or fail him in a way
he would understand, but I never will.

2.

Among the towns and cities where he stopped to read his poems,
those who did not know him perhaps found similar surprises: sober
husbands came home in cheerfulness, the dog brought the paper to the
front door, kaleidoscopic neighbors dimmed.

In Charlottesville, he lay in his bed, empty of industry,
except for the cancer cells still working to make sure he would
not return to his desk, to his martial, loud shoes, and elegant rings,
and the laughter, the sly intelligence, and silly jokes enchanting
a world far beyond the one in which he lived.

We, who were the business of his hands, collapsed,
soughed in a raw emptiness.
Or hurried into rooms of meaningless tedium.
No telephones would ring again
with him.
No dashed notes begin in
bold letters on a yellow field.

The correspondence of our lives became mute.

My New Agent

Once, every day I nuzzled
a gun to my soft palate. I
remember the taste of the barrel:
sassy steel and sweet linseed.

I would have done it,
but somehow thought of
you, though we had not met,
only spoken on the phone.

But it was enough, knowing
that you liked, no, you loved
Jack Manning and hated to
"Let him go

back into the pages, into those
long, beautiful lines I read
in my office, until the twilight
of the City made it too dark."

Who could pop into oblivion
with such tender conversation?

Druid

I have seen the winter trees
with empty, black limbs
and I love it for this.

I relish the clarity
which comes with nothing.
I embrace all that isn't

and say come to me.
I will heal and make
you lush and rich and
noisy with golden bees.

Teressa

Under the bright
bow of the moon
I have crept out
to my nanny's grave
to swirl her up
from the dead. I don't believe
in magic, yet here I am
with a root doctor,
two pieces of a preacher's skull,
the comb of a black guinea hen,
and the webbed feet
of an orange terrapin—all
to summon the only one
whose love embraced me
like a jasmine apron.

Forbearance

In the library, I check my watch—
four o'clock, time to stop
reading bad poetry. Time
to go home and boil
potatoes so they'll be soft
and sweet by five.
Ready to dab with
butter and jam
down my throat
with bloody meat
and milk and Klonopin.
Get it all down before
dark so I don't gulp
gin until it makes my heart
stutter, pound, and twitch
like some ancient engine
ready to blow.

The Mackerel Fishers

Apparel is anatomy. Take a trip. Keep notes.
—George Garrett

How I wish I could say
they wore deer hide boots
and black, oiled slickers

and odd hats with long flaps
to keep away the flies
as they fished along the pier.

How I wish I could say
they were hard, lean men,
smokers, all red faces

above windblown beards
bristle white in August mist
their voices silent on the tide.

But the mackerel fishers
in Eastport were not these rough
portraits I couldn't forget.

They were just like me,
wearing blue jeans, athletic shoes,
baseball hats, their bodies too fat.

Not one of them smoked
or wore thrilling beards
and all complained about
first wives and odd moles.

James Dickey's Last Assignment

"Now write me some immortal line."
Though lasting words could not be mine,
it was a fine instruction.
I knew this last assignment told
me much about your end: behold
the poet's cold submission.

Duet

Your life mask I keep before me,
but not at the center of my desk.
It sits beside a box of paper
scraps, the pieces spotted with ink:
words trying to become

something. Since I hate things not balanced
I sometimes move it to the proper place—
right in the clutter of my work,
but I cannot leave it here
even for a while.

I push it again to the side,
put your wry aluminum face
in eraser dust and shavings,
thinking: how silly, we are finished
you and I.

Churchill's Contrition

Bethlehem, now I hear you weeping
in the Church of the Nativity:
the steeple gunfire rules the city
and mocks the sound of bells keeping

the holy hours. If such terror can
invade this sacred darkness where light
supposedly was born, then no might
may resist it, no fortress of man.

And yet it was my own endeavor,
justice, that made this land forever
a place of evisceration.

Bethlehem, you have a bloody scent.
Oh little town, should I now repent
my careful theft to build a nation?

Madam Curie's Notebooks

In lead-lined boxes to properly shield us
your notebooks lay, their vigor still unquelled.
Some say they glow. Have any pages held
literally the power to kill? We can fuss

with diction all day, but your books will rot flesh
from the bones of anyone who reads them.
To know that my words could actually condemn
my gentle reader, snatch away the fresh

lust of pretty eyes, deplete the full breath—
oh, God, I would risk eternal death
to deliver such a catastrophe

with only words. So now you think I'm insane—
most of you, but not the writers who remain
wild to leave some incandescent legacy.

Defeat

After the best effort has failed
there should be cool acceptance:
writing letters to old friends,
an overdue visit to Mass,
long naps in the afternoon.

This is the way failure should be
swallowed. Somehow it does not go
that way for me. There comes a frantic,
furious denial, then countless
attempts to win to win to win
until finally I sprawl stunned at

the bottom, more bludgeoned by
my obstinacy than the stinging blow.

Why can't I take it like
a long and elegant shave?

Recognition

Before Christmas, the light
in the country church was cold,
but the congregation sat as far
apart as ever. Reverend Hitch
rose with the sermon: we should
think of others. Adopt a convict
from the nearby prison. Afterwards,
my parents steamy and sweet with
booze accepted my plea.

We met him beneath a bare walnut
tree outside the bars. He was young
and good looking. My father hated
him for gaping at Mama. When he brushed
his hand through my hair, he shattered
the pane of my heart.

Frost

Even when I was a kid
I saw the black thread
weaving through the
words.

Nothing was ever
simple and true,
though you tried
to sell it that way.

Every thin birch
and long drip
of ice—the petals
of spring flowers—bore
your bleak stitch.

I wonder where it
finally pulled you:
the oblivion
you so feared
or a hell forged perfectly

in your cold mind,
some kind of icy
beauty smoldering
at the core.

Southern Snow

The small snow of winter descends
and the magnolia apprehends
the truth: it bends with cold grace
for this frozen falling is rare,
will vanish with sun into air
leaving no care or harsh trace.

The Wind in May

In May I start to enter late
and slow beneath the oaks,
to watch wind shake the leaves
and to listen to it rattle slate
of houses near the campus.

I stay as long as I can keep
my waiting low, not obvious,
as if I'm happy with the spring.
I cough to prove I'm not asleep,
just pausing here before I go

to class and final duties there.
I call the roll, but do not look;
I make my voice sound light with ease
for through the years I've learned to bear
this departure deceptively.

After you have left the room,
I remain and hear your voices,
laughing down the hollow stairs.
The wind in May presages gloom.

Te Deum

When I was brimming at the lip
for you, any sleight beauty
would spill me over: a white gate
wide open, the fibrillation
and shimmer of deep minnows,
a daisy gold in two petals,
the taste of M&Ms in one
mouthful, then guzzled down with
popping Coke. Any of these things
and a million others would make
my adolescent self shout out
thanksgivings to you, God. Bring me
to that effervescence once more
until I boil and empty
into inexhaustible depths.

Earthquake in Peru

Beneath the orphanage
something more than earth
slips. Sleeping like the others,

I am sucked down deep,
the hole taking everyone
in this cursed house.

Like the others I sink
silently as if we orphans
have no right to scream

until my lungs blacken
and fill with what I will become,
am becoming.

Oh, little ones,
you who wait, airless, still, mute—

Lord, where is my breath?

Providence

I like to learn the way of things
how they fit or break apart
how a bit tears into steel.
The glory of a lock.

I like to learn the way of things
and not just the tool and die
but how a bass fans out a nest
how a man will die—

Then live

to fly on rainbow wings
and sail beyond the dark
as if it were a certainty
that the way of things is art.

The Lovely Prescription

It seemed always in the summer
I would take my grandfather's
warm black book. Soft as the flesh
of his hands, and sit beneath
a menthol of green leaves
reading the underlined words
he preached on Sunday.

Scripture was my remission
from the abuse of my parents,
the craze of my half-born heart,
the overwhelming apprehension
life was something about to burst.

In those medicinal afternoons
I was relieved of all these fears,
assuaged by ancient miracles:
David and his little sling;
Daniel lounging among the cats;
Shadrak, Meshak, and Abednego.

So now when things feel ominous,
I take off walking to the woods,
holding that soft and heavy book,
reading again those Sunday stories,
letting leaves fill this lovely prescription.

Below

Now
I move
stealthily
behind my house,
studying the ground
deep in summer debris:
avalanches of leaves dry
in the turning light. Out West, fall
broods softly in the great yellow plains
where the temperature tries to reach forty.
Some creatures are digging in my backyard. They
push up beach sand which balances like white castles
across the grass. Something else is making perfect holes
beside the sharp holly. Though I cannot catch the diggers
in their secret industry, the magic work makes me feel glad.

Reunion

Since it is formal
I prepare for my
visit with proper clothes:
sweats and stocking cap
white socks and black gloves.

Arriving, I punch play.
Rocky vibrates their stones,
sends black crows away
while above my head
I lift my gloved hands

triumphantly. I dance
across their red clay bones,
the golden wedding rings
and plastic teeth, singing
my own victory:

Dead. Dead. All of you dead
deep in the skinny red earth
and I am as fat as
a butter-fed cat
out of the reach of your hurt.

A Pornographer's Lament

Let all my good words beg apology
for the other ones gone bad
which scratched or dug into the page sins
that might compel a boy
to dream some lusciousness: like
catching some brown beauty in ecstasy
before her image in a stream
and from behind taking her fiercely
as he reads in his bed
my words by light beneath a quilt.

I should make them praise beautifully
the one and only voice I know
to make the blacker parts of print light
but words refuse to go
like me any way but their own.

Half Pint

A mean June sun.
I'm hungover real bad.
Down the street, a boy
comes running, comes crying.
He's two feet high with
a blue diving mask
on his head, yellow trunks, barefoot.

I don't wanna talk, but say:
"What's the matter?"
His moonless black eyes swallow.
"They won't let me in 'cause
it cost five dollar."
I got it, but I need a hard half pint.
Otherwise, I'm hurtin' all day.

Someway, my hand shakes
a fiver to him. His long hug
spots my jeans with tears.
I watch him run down
the blistering street
to
his
cool
heaven.

Night Baseball

for James Dickey

Slouching in the bleachers,
your father is here—
a player once, one-eyed.
Shutmouth guy, hands like liver.
You remember his forearms
wrapped around you
holding the bat.

Tonight, eight years later
you got his style:
a chaw, nothing to say,
hair blond as biscuit.
Eyes long-ball blue.

Oh, there were other games
in bumpy lots—
milkweed and rusting cars—
but not like this.
This is it tonight:
stinging summer,
your first little league.

When you step up
you look at him,
but he doesn't.
He just spits.
So do you
and tap your cleats
the way you saw him do.

The night is day
but not quite.
Darkness lies curled
in the pitcher's mix.

You dig your cleats,
look one last time,
and now he looks too,
his one eye hard
with expectation.

And it comes,
the first one, white and fast
and so hot
it makes you blink.
And braver
than any could guess, you
drop your chin, judging
wrong.
Taking the clean curve
above your heart.

Somehow I am there
behind you
and feel the dreadful ball
shatter your chest,
dropping you,
watching you go down,
smiling, unafraid
down to the red dust
dying
dead.

Your father scowls,
hands cupped about his mouth,
shouting: Get up, damn you, get up!

Now I shift.
My iridescent wings extending,

spreading out, sheltering you,
in what has been given me
the secret
no one can resist or know,
and release it
feeling your cells swarm
back toward light.

You blink, shiver, struggle
reaching towards me
until I lift you
boy of dust
breathing
rising
sure
to play
better than him
better than anybody
tonight.

Glue

May is my disintegration.
The classroom holds only light
and the gloom that summer brings:
empty buildings, empty life.

My very person shows the change—
ink of essays fades away
from my lessoned fingertips, while
my clothes deteriorate

to greasy T-shirts, riven pants.
Soon I do not bathe or brush;
it is too much to clean my nails
or cut my burgeoning beard.

A campus cop asks who I am.
"Tomatoes," I would like to say
but my woes he could never see,
nor the cure in my garden

planted in spring. Tall and sunny,
young and trim, the tomato vines
slow my grim dissolution.
I disappear among them,

until the last of summer haze
when my students start oozing in.
The young glue sticks me together,
and I am I again.

A Teacher's Discovery

I would not let you fall in love with me
though you wanted to because I found
the music. The craze and crack of your words
I read that winter morning I will always
hear. And because I told you: look,
look at this. Look at what you have done.
Incredible. Your hands grabbed mine and brought
them to your mouth wet as half a peach
to kiss, knowing the agonies
of your life now had meaning: a poem
with such incomprehensible edge
that all who press it open and bleed
at last understand their own sickness,
spilling it out luxuriously,
pouring it out hotly, madly, dreamily
until there is only one sense remaining:
the emptiness of the healed.

Peregrinations

I hear the tub drinking
night after night   gulping, huffing water
down
as if it has been on a long
journey   the four fat legs
scuttling
to some place else.

Maybe it leaves the room
when I leave   slipping
the rusty pipes which
hold it tight   and creeping out
the house
a way only
tubs know.

Then returning exhausted
from the long ramble
plugging back in   cinching and screwing
to wait for me   consumed with obedience
and ineffable
thirst.

Comedy

When I see the trees shake with wind
it makes me think they have a joke
they cannot keep among themselves
so toss it to the nearest friend
in hopes that he will play along.

Today must be a belly roll:
it seems all the woods are shaking.
The pines and pecans catch the news
and soon the oaks and poplars toll
some lusty gag of spring.

I think the trees are watching me.
Perhaps they'd like to share a laugh.
How I'd love to take them up
and laugh with them about something
only we can understand.

Catherine the Great

For a three-person tea party
Grandmother opened the banquet table
to fourteen feet long, five wide
and laid out all her Georgian flatware,
263 pieces all shining like a tsar's teeth.
When it was over, Teressa reported a pie
cutter was missing. Beaming in her April,
Grandmother said: oh, how she must have coveted it!

Up the Trees

Cicadas are awake again
from thirteen years of sleep.

They slide and skirl across the leaves.
They jump from boughs and trunks

to cut along some gnarly limbs
so all the air's a-screech.

Cacophony evokes a kind
of fear or sleeping dread

as if disaster waits for me,
a terror dim and deep.

All noise does this, not just their own
predicted fizz and din.

I'll soon get taken to the bin,
but not today. I'll sleep.

Fugitive

I hear it as I close the door
to the men's room: a slither
and rasp like something
in the dry woods. And even
though I tell myself it is not
possible for one to be here—
a place of tile and porcelain
and rattling fans—still I think it lies
just to my right, thick and slow,
hot to strike, as if after
a long hunt it has found me
for what I did to the others.
To soothe myself I say:
there are none in public places,
then leave this stinking room
wearing one of many faces
I have for sanity.

Starry Men

Bloody toothpicks in my pocket
more than remind me of you—
it is you, this habit, picking
at my gums after meals, though
I think your digging was not
cleanliness, but something darker:
always hurt yourself, Daddy.
Usually more deeply, carving
your bony legs with little stars
and letting me count them until
I cut them too: meteors
falling from my knees to ankles
made me feel I could anesthetize
my life.

It took us a long time to know
a hard truth: the world will not abate
for starry men its agitation
no matter how diligently
we whittle our gentle flesh
hoping by small cuts to make
the big ones bearable.

Ease

Sometimes my prayers are short
they stop above my head
and God must bend to lift
the ones which I have pled
not nearly hard enough.

But when I think again
about my little pleas
is it some kind of sin
to offer them with ease?

I'm getting old, not long to live.
I hold my life above a sieve.

Aunt Elizabeth

In the morning   the very earliest quietest part
of the morning   when even birds seemed   to wish
the dim oblivion of their sleep   but a little longer
I heard the chords   of Rimsky-Korsakov   from the vast piano
of the house   so vast it cannot   even today   be removed
from the music room   as you practiced   for the recital
in Moscow   which would decide your fate   in the world   of notes.

Even at eight   I remember   how much you wished
to impress Prokofiev   how much   you yearned   to be great
so that everyone in the house   swelled
with your expectation   even the oranges (you said)   Grandfather
and Grandmother's faces   found color unseen for years   shining
like pomegranates   Teressa and Bub and Tee-Tat bursting
with your hope to equal   or at least impress, no stun
the Russian maestro   who (you said) was no pianist.

But your Scheherazade   opus 35   never left the house
because you collapsed, descending   into twitches and giggles
confessing   Moscow was too cold.

Beneath a Yankee Bridge

The day you heard it, we were drunk
and bleeding from our soles,
shooting hoops beside your house
barefoot for some reason.
I'm sure it was the booze
that numbed our feet to ooze
upon the cement.

The call came from some northern state,
and Maxine held the phone
staring at our wounded feet
so bloody were the prints.
It's something bad, she slurred
as you embraced the words:
his head busted the ice.

I recall the simplicity—
you bared your gappy teeth
and flicked your tongue across them
relishing response,
then said to me cold as lead
"John Berryman is dead
beneath a Yankee bridge."

What followed then I can't forget,
a cheerful cruelty:
"W.B. Yeats of dead Swinburne said—
'And now I'm king of cats.'"
Just twenty-one, I sat
learning the trade.

Chaplain FDNY

Father Judge lies dead upon the white altar
of St. Paul's Church, placed here by firemen
for whom his gin eyes were always full of prayer.
Stretched out in ashes in his last amen,

he does not seem dead, but rather puzzled
at the interruption of his work:
        Is this some dream bed, or me passed out on
the altar saying the Mass too long?

My heart failing me, and the boys sticking
me here before the Tabernacle in
a true honor? He stops. Smoking sheets
are borne into the church. He remembers:

        I see them again. They jump. They hold
each other's hands, furiously
striking the street, men and women.
What rain is this that falls in human flesh?

He awakes, rising, stepping towards corpses,
hands searching sooty pockets for Holy oil.
Softly applying it to skin which remains
he whispers: "Nunc dimittis, Domine . . ."

Carnage

At night I cannot bear the road.
By five I ease into my mode:
with gin I load my old sink
and drink a cup against the street
where deer and skunks and foxes meet
a raw, concrete death. I drink.

Remains

The paint on a table
sitting on our porch—
several different colors—
brown on blue on white.
This is what remains
of the great house
I grew up in.

I love this table and
right now wonder
why I've allowed it
to be relegated to
the sun and weather.

It deserves something.
What? By my bed where
it sat for years, as it
also sat by my mother's?

When I put it outside, black
cigarette burns littered
the brown last coat.

Mother's recklessness
always came to mind.
But somehow the elements
removed them leaving
only slick pecan.

I think a few days,
then strip it and
set it in my room,
shining like newborn
bone.

A Ghost Observes His Grave

I always lived
a look away
from you and them
and all of it.
So studying
my new marker,
a copper plate shining
beneath the moon,
it's just right
to be a bag
of white dust buried
on the edge of
the busy cemetery.

Reoccurrence

Bust out the morphine and the Tattinger,
tap the Demerol and chill the Mumms.
Liberate the chocolates from their tinsel nests,
sauce the pork, free bourbon from the drums.

Let the long-anticipated party
begin. Invite the dour oncologists
who were sure I would die their tedious
death of chemotherapy. Nope. My wrists

remain pale and soft and inviolate.
Strong enough to pop a cork, or whip cream
so thick that strawberries bounce and glitter.
I drink. I laugh. I eat. Death is a dream.

Seasons of the Killer

To murder in spring
takes very little courage:
life is abundant.

June is my illness.
The terrible heat slows me.
I hide from the sun.

Leaves yellow and fall
into piles of fragile death.
I hunt in the cold.

The winter moon smiles
having seen me. Is she dead?
I hold her white face.

A Warning

Some are slender,
others broad and blunt.
Most the way you would think:
cut and worn and tough,
battered at the tip and thin
at the heel. All fallen from
some incomprehensible tree
into a pile: blue and tan,
black and brown, but others
yellow, violet, even pink
with frail, satin fibers
or frilled gauze knit
in the abyss
of that time.

In Jerusalem, they
crowd a wooden box
roaring in silence
a new warning.

Will anyone hear
the million little shoes of Yad Vashem?

Couple Dies in Plane Crash

I throw the yellow roses from your birthday
in the backyard where the young deer have lain
through these cold Yankee nights. The grass is long
because we did not let the boy cut it
and all summer in the mornings it was flat
and white because of their sleeping. Yellow
roses on white grass is pretty, but it
makes me uneasy to do this. I should keep them
even though we are leaving Maine today
on the plane for home. You say it doesn't
matter, but both of us feel that it does,
as if throwing away something so
delicate, so much a part of this special
day might curse you or us. We do not believe
in superstitions except in the greatest
one of all, but we stand and stare until
we cannot bear it and I gather
them up and come inside rolling them
in wax paper through which a thorn sticks me
drawing blood. One drop splatters across
these faces hidden in their thin missile.
Carefully, I wipe it off, packing
the delicate roll in my suitcase.
We hold one another and feel as though
something has been avoided.

The Other Way

So this is what all your horror meant, Mother: neglect.
You had tried with goodness to arouse everyone's attention
and, yes, love: the susurration of your voice; the feigned
cheerfulness of your spirit; salubrious advice; a gentle glance;
a full embrace; winks. None of it works. Everyone still ignored
you until you went the other way: wheezing, coughing, shrieks,
maniacal laughs, personalities raised out of hell.

What tenderness could not acquire you found through
        shape-shifting.

Oh, Mama, once I picked you violent flowers until my eyes
swelled shut.

Beauty with Script

This morning, I'm eating
fried eggs and baloney
because I want it.

Besides, I'm taking Crestor.
Can't hurt my arteries, right?
Just my liver.

I go to the IGA
and buy Oscar Mayer
and double-yolk eggs.

The Indian girl slouches
behind the register.
Across her ebony chest
gleam black tats.

I think Passamaquoddy language:
Children of the Dawn, perhaps.

But the gloomy bagboy says
he dated her
it's Chinese and means:
"Party till you puke."

Sewing Bees

My daughter wears a sash of bees.
Their golden bodies ring her waist,
and through the abdomen of each
and passing out the head
there runs a silver vein.

I wonder how she learned this craft
of sewing bees together with
a needle and her mother's thread.

I dream of honeybees at night
and watch my little girl unfold
unfeeling hands that catch her sting.
I try to blow them from the pane.

The Silver Plate

In my bureau drawer   my father's ring   boils

blue as his eye   sometimes I think it watches   me
and if rings exhort   it says   why don't you   hunt

the one   who took   a tool   and   hammered

until he busted through   the silver plate

implanted   to protect   and my brains

spilled out   like cooked apples

beneath   the astonished   moon.

Restoril

Daddy, please forgive my ten-year-old
condemnation. I understand now
why after school I would find you in bed,
missing work again, your blue eyes boiling
with fear, the flesh beneath black as your
dyed moustache, swallowing pill after pill—
Seconal, though not one or all of them putting
you to sleep, simply keeping you together
while something tore at you relentlessly
and your little holy candles blinked, filling
the rooms with the smell of Mass: beeswax
and myrrh.

I thought you so weak, so pathetic, so bony
in your single, peeling bed so far from Mom's
while I at ten felt superior, promising myself
I'd never be like you and yet here I am in my
single bed far from any woman, swallowing
Restoril at 2:00 PM, trying to keep myself
sane, until horror fades away, and I
can leave bed for work to find a place where
fear cannot.

It looked much better than this. Some artist drew it
the way they do with lines that are never straight
and curves that have something else in them like
breath, or some inscrutable motion.
On a cement wall it was yellow for the trunk,
green for the canopy and even a brown knot
whirling in a lovely way which seemed without
effort. Beneath this tree was one word, stamped,
not written, in black paint: PLANT.
I drew up close thinking it was a definition,
only to realize that it was not that at all—
it was a command. Plant! Go plant! An injunction
to the world. To all who are green. To all who are not
green. To me.
I smiled the whole day
filling the earth with forests.

Three Writers

Richard Eberhart

Tonight I remembered him. I was twenty-five.
        He was about sixty. We were
drinking not too much in a bar. I told him I
        was having my first affair—a blonde
with a big sunhat. He said it was good it was a
        girl, then told me about tutoring
the King of Siam whose kisses tasted like the
        seeds of pomegranates.

When I asked him about God, he said
        sometimes he parked his reason with his
car beside a curb and went into the church.

Berhard Malamud

He was walking up a green hill at Bennington
        with a seraglio following. I yelled
across the distance: Do you believe in God?
        God, he said, yes. Do you believe
in a God who knows about the death of every
        sparrow? He stopped, looked
down, smiled. Sparrows, he said—very small
        birds.

Conrad Aiken

I was in Savannah finishing a novel when
      someone called to take me to meet Mary Aiken
in a hovel on a side street, she made us
      martinis in a red and silver thermos jug.
She told me when Conrad was dying, she
      would bring him his martinis in the
thermos to get past the nurses. She also
      brought their special olives—Spanish
ones, I believe. On his last day, she mixed a
      drink.

He gulped it and made a face. "Bad olive, my dear."
      Then died.

Doubt

Send me an angel
to batter down my doubt
who shines—scalding,
pure as a new
child who will have
no mercy upon me, saying:
abandon your questions—
all is grandeur.

Deliquescence

I can't look at open cupboards.
It makes me feel sick, as if I'm disintegrating:
rice leaking from a bag, a lonely drip of syrup,
sugar spilled like secret frost,
dead roach, live roach, scattered toothpicks,
open cereal bags, flakes of oatmeal.
I close every door.

The Fever in Soweto

2001

Sex with a virgin will cure you of AIDS
the infected say in South Africa.
Children, do not play beyond your parents'
eyes: the thin man is hunting tonight.

Where did he find you, little Tombi?
Were you dancing beneath the Baobab?
Or catching a bee to throw at your friends?
Though only nine, the skeleton took you

out of childhood into his dread disease.
Sweating with fever, tens of thousands pray
us to deliver the bright cocktail,
but the Minister of Health forbids it.

Her words: "Too much money. Unproven."
Sometimes even the oppressed are guilty.
Run like the wind, Tombi, gazelles will comfort
you in the wandering softness of herds.

And what of us, in our cool opulence?
Will we withdraw, sour with spells and darkness?
We should grieve each hour for a solution—
or plead: Mandela, Mandela, Mandela.

The Last Time I Blushed at a Story of Yours

Lowell Thomas I never believed you knew   though you
claimed it   and that he liked you wanted you   in the forties
to work for him   years later we watched *Lawrence of Arabia*
he made him you said   who made who? Thomas made T.E.
Lawrence into Lawrence of Arabia.

But I did come to believe on that day in 1970 when Mister
Thomas   all teeth and broad-brimmed hat his string tie
clipped with a fiery opal stopped at Columbia to visit his
archive   and I in a Mickey Mouse shirt and sandals   my
young body sculpted beautiful by weights   yelled through the
fawning professors and confused legislators   who voted five
million to buy and preserve Thomas' work   I yelled my dad
was Ben Greer   and he yelled back you look like him   and I
blushed like a child, hearing you again.

James Dickey's Lot

Only the written word remains.
           —Horace

So I will start with the end:
staring at lights on water,
a dock that will not give
beneath your feet again.

Of your time there is not one
thing left here, not one gray brick
of the narrow, low house
at whose roof I for fun

dared to throw rocks, a boy
in love with poetry.

Or was it for fame I threw?
You were truly famous then,
all the critics agree.
My raw intellect knew

the answer to your question:
"Because I love symmetry,"
I said, and saw you smile
at awkward deception.

Back then I did not know
deception was your truth

and became mine for long years,
allowing us to spar in
perfect syncopation
through football, class, and beers.

Now beneath the owl-held tree
you lie deep in root light,
while standing on your lot
staring is only me

stricken by the ancient line:
Littera scripta manet.

Solace

2008

On January eleventh
snow puzzles Baghdad
and Death escapes its common work.

Seventy years ago the old
say they saw it last—
heavy sky falling like cotton.

The mortar shells cease whistling
across the Green Zone.
Busy checkpoints in Qom are clear.

For the first time in five years
blood stays in its place—
the limbed bodies of sane men.

No envoys meet to consider.
The streets all turn white.
Snow confounds the desert war.

My Little Celebration

Today is my wedding anniversary   the bees dance in thyme
birds remember old melodies   even gnats mass and
sing   in round, floating notes   all little life is overcome
with the love   of my love
with the surprise of an old man   come
late to the riches   of a wife and child
who dissolve my wounds   like nectar in their mouths.

An Honest Place to Stand

for Billy Collins

Among the mad
I have found
my solace.
Among those who
cannot tell
one beauty
from the rest:
a canary from
a daffodil; a knife
from a blade
of grass.

Ben Greer was born in Spartanburg, South Carolina, on December 4, 1948. He was raised in the magical hamlet of Glenn Springs. He graduated from the University of South Carolina and Hollins University. He published his first novel, *Slammer*, at twenty-six to rave reviews and went on to publish four others. His first book of poetry was published at fifty-nine. Ben has also written three plays, including *Little Tin Gods*, produced by Theatre South in 2008. Having taught at the University of South Carolina for thirty-three years, he is retired and divides his time between South Carolina and Maine.

CPSIA information can be obtained
at www.ICGtesting.com
Printed in the USA
BVHW031607171120
593551BV00003B/153